Plan your wedding
your way

One of the questions I am asked most frequently is 'where do I start'! The purpose of this planning guide is to assist you through the process. I have broken down each of the items that you will need to organise.

Don't worry if you don't stick to this religiously, or if you don't have a need for some of the items I mention. This is your wedding day and you can do what is right for you. This is an assistance guide and not intended as a 'Must Do'.

Plan your wedding day your way!

I always recommend starting as you mean to go on. By that I mean, starting a spread sheet to keep your budget under control. There will be a lot of moving parts that you will need to manage. Visit irishweddingblog.ie to download my free sample wedding budget template.

When you start to compile your potential guest list, set up an additional tab on your budget spread sheet. Over time, you can update with RSVP details, log addresses and make note of gifts etc. This list will also be the foundation of your table plan. It's worth your while grouping people in their significant groups, that way when it comes to your table plan, you will be able to start picking your 8-10 per table.

It is also worth your while starting a secret Pinterest board. You can log all your inspirations and ideas here so that you have your pictures to hand. It is so handy when you go for make-up and hair trials.

xoxo

Sara Kennedy

06

15

12

08

10

04

14

Contents

Decide on what your wedding day will look like

When do you want to get married?

Time of year can affect the style, right through to budget. It is important to a have a rough idea of what time of year you would prefer. You may also find that there are price differences between peak times of year versus slower months. You also need to decide if you are open to a mid-week or is it a set weekend or even a specific date that you want.

What type of venue or location are you thinking of?

Once you know the size of your wedding, you can start to rule out certain venues or locations. By type of venue I mean; castle, hotel, stately home etc. Location could be abroad or within Ireland.

Example of what could be established:

* Winter Wedding.
* Friday or Saturday night.
* 100-120 guests – no more than 140 and no less than 80.
* Venue such as castle or stately home.
* Budget is total €20,000 including honeymoon.

How many people do you want to bring?

Ah yes, the ultimate debate! Here is where the first wedding quarrel can rear its ugly head either between yourselves or your families! You will need to decide if you both want a big or small wedding. Once you start to think about size, start logging all names in a spread sheet. This will be your blue print to coordinating your budget, table plan and invitation list.

Do you have a budget in mind?

This question works in tandem with the previous questions as what you want and what you can afford. These are two very different things! At this point you may want to start to think about how much you can both save. What do you have saved already? Will you need financial support from family? Or will you need a loan? You may not know how much to expect to pay, but once you start shopping for your wedding items such as venue and band, you will start to get an idea and then establish if it is affordable.

Once you have answered the initial questions, you should have a better idea of what you want. This allows you to focus your time more effectively.

Now try to create your wedding day!

Chapter One

Ceremony

There are two ceremony options available; religious or non-religious. With all options, I would advise that you get a selection of dates and then check with your venue for availability. If you confirm a date with your ceremony provider and then cannot find a venue for the same date, it will add to your work load.

Religious

If you decide that the church option is for you, here are the steps to get you through the process:

(Please note that I have based this on a catholic ceremony. Church of Ireland and other religious ceremony procedures may vary.)

1. Choose your preferred church.
2. Schedule an appointment with the residing priest. Talk to that priest/minister and ask him for available dates/times and if he is available to do the ceremony or if you need to bring your own priest/minister.
3. Confirm the date and time and he will pencil you in.
4. If you or your fiancé is from another parish, you will need to get a letter of release from your parish priest. You just need to call them, tell them you need one and visit the office and collect. Now, this can be easier said than done as I had to get a letter from three parishes that I lived in! I had moved apartments twice in one year, plus I was registered in my parents parish. My fiancé was meant to do the same but he got a tip that you can get your local solicitor to write a clearance letter that will cover you regardless of parish.
5. You will need to notify the state three months before the wedding date. I recommend doing this at least four months before your wedding date. The last thing you want to do is leave this last minute. Follow the steps outlined in notifying the state.
6. Once you get your certificate from the registrar, you will give this to your priest/minister upon your next visit.
7. If opting for a catholic ceremony, you will be required do a pre-marriage course. You must show that certificate to your priest. Some priests can have a preference for the different agencies.

8. You will need to get your priest to proof read your mass booklet to ensure that your readings and ceremony for the event are correct.

9. Once you gather your certificates, you will then have your appointment with your priest and he will do the Pre-Nuptial form with you.

From that point the priest looks after everything. You will sign your certificate on the day and then your priest will submit your paperwork and the state will be notified that you have been married.

Once married, you will then be able to apply and get your marriage cert. If you would like to change your maiden name to your married name, you will need this certificate to do so.

Pre-Marriage Course

If you are having a religious ceremony, your priest will insist that you complete the pre marriage course. Some non-religious celebrants may also recommend that you and your partner complete this course.

There are two types of course, you can do a class over a few evenings or a one-day course.

Vendors that run these courses include Accord and Avalon. There are other vendors available too. I took the full day Avalon course and I couldn't recommend it enough. Initially, I was hesitant about doing the course as I had heard that they can be very religion heavy and slightly archaic. I was proved wrong. The course was very focused on relationships.

At the start, the religious sacrament of marriage was discussed but we were straight in to relationship discussions with an actual relationship therapist. She gave great insight in to the key reasons why marriages can break down. We were introduced to better ways to communicate and were made think about real issues that could come up and how we would cope. There were issues that we never thought about such as, if one of our parents were sick would they live with us? Do we want children and if so, how many?

I felt the benefit of the course and was so happy that in the madness of planning our wedding day, we got time to focus on our relationship which will benefit us for life.

Non-Religious

Civil Ceremony with HSE

You can get married with the General Registrar in either a registry office or approved location as per the HSE. You don't need to live in the location from which you want to get married. The registrar must be on the Registrar of Solemnisers.

Like the religious ceremony previously mentioned, you will also need to notify the state at minimum 3 months prior to your wedding date. Follow the steps advised in 'Notifying the State'.

There are a few items worth noting should you wish to get married outside of the registry office:

✴ Ceremonies can only take place Monday – Friday. It excludes bank holidays and public holidays.

✴ The location must be in a place that is "open to the public" as per the HSE. This means:
   a. *"A building that is open to the public, or*
   b. *A courtyard, garden, field or piece of ground that is open to the public and lying near to and usually enjoyed with the building"*

In other words – it can't be your back garden……unless that's open to the public!

There are details relating to health and safety, insurance, accessibility and religious connection that are checked. Details in to the criteria for approval can be found on the HSE website.

✴ Most hotels are approved by the HSE for ceremonies but always ask when booking. If the venue is not approved, you will need to request a visitation for approval. Allow plenty of time for this as this is not a quick process.

✴ There is an approximate fee of €200 to have the registrar marry you outside of the registry office.

Civil Ceremony – Humanist Type

Humanists work independent of the HSE registrars. You can expect a fee of approximately €300 upwards. There could be travel expenses too. The great thing about a humanist is that they are not restricted by the HSE ceremony times. They will facilitate weekends and holidays.

Tip

You can order your marriage certificate online from www.hse.ie/eng/services/list/1/bdm/Certificates/

The booking and processing of a humanist ceremony follows the same criteria as the HSE registrar. You will still need to notify the state as per the steps advised in the 'Notifying the state' section.

Civil Partnerships

A civil partnership is the provision for same sex couples. In terms of the paper work and legalities, the procedure follows the same as civil ceremony.

Notifying the State

Applies to all wedding types

To book this appointment you can log on to:
www.hse.ie/eng/services/list/1/bdm/crsappointment/

When you go to your appointment you will need the following:

- ✔ €200
- ✔ Both Passports
- ✔ Original Birth Cert and a Photocopy
- ✔ Utility Bill with Proof of Address
- ✔ PPS Number Proof
- ✔ Names & Dates of Birth of Both Witnesses
- ✔ Name & Address of Priest

At this appointment you will be given a certificate which you need to hand the priest/humanist/registrar/celebrant for your next visit.

From that point your priest/humanist/registrar/celebrant will look after everything. You will sign your certificate on the day and they will submit all of your paperwork and the state will be notified that you are ready.

You will then be able to apply and get your marriage cert if you would like to change your maiden name to your married name.

Chapter Two

This is where the main part of your budget is going to go,
so it is important that you are armed with the
right questions and considerations.

When couples used to arrive in to the venues I represented, they arrived like rabbits caught in headlights and had this big hill of information to overcome. I would recommend that you prepare before each visit so that you can organise the information accordingly. It makes it a lot easier to compare all venues after your visit.

The majority of the time, if a couple likes the look and feel of a venue they will book on that basis alone! I recommend putting your game face on. If a sales person suspects that you are a done deal, they won't give as good a discount. If you are non-emotional, you might have a better negotiating position.

Couples would present themselves as almost apologetic and this is not a good state of mind to be in when visiting venues. You need to remember that you are about to spend some serious money with the venue you select. It should be the venue that is nervous as it is crucial for them to get your business. You may not be familiar with how a wedding works but you are the client.

The main thing to do is to book a wedding show around with the best person and one with whom you will be dealing with for the duration of your wedding planning. You should ask who this will be when you phone for your appointment. It is crucial that you meet the correct person and not someone standing in for them. You will find that most venues will have a wedding coordinator that will look after all of your requirements. Some wedding venues have a coordinator that looks after everything until the month before and then hands over to the banqueting manager. Generally, a banqueting manager runs the event on the day. You will have a file so it is important that your records and requests are maintained properly so that the banqueting manager can clearly see what you need.

Steps

1 Finding a venue

I get many emails every week asking me to recommend venues to brides and grooms to be. I come back with the following questions so that I can give them the best advice:

* Numbers
* Budget per head
* Time of year
* Venue type preference / style e.g. castle, contemporary hotel
* Venue specifications – i.e. does it need to be a certain distance from your home or airport?
* Does it need to have certain features?

From that list I can generally find a suitable venue. I suggest that every couple considers this.

Once you have built the picture of what you want, it makes your search easier. In terms of selecting which venues to visit, I would start with aiming to review a maximum of 10 venues by paper/phone. This is where you go to their website, read their information, look at the brochures and then phone the hotel to establish if it's in keeping with your criteria. Look for real examples of weddings that took place in your selected wedding venue. This will give you a good indication on what it really looks like for a wedding day.

When you phone, this is almost like a pre-screening. Only certain lucky candidates will make it through to the next round!

Here are some pointers for your phone call:

a. Do not commit to visiting or holding a date on the first call.
b. The person on the other end of your call will have an objective

to get you to come in for a show around. Before committing to a visit, you should have a list of questions

c. Your questions should confirm that they meet the criteria outlined in point 1. You should ask about availability and if there are special offers.

d. They will ask for your email, phone number and address so that they can send you a pack and to keep your details on file for following up.

e. Most venues will not give you dates over the phone and you will need to go to the hotel to get dates and to provisionally book dates.

f. They will push to get you to book a show around. Hold off booking on the first phone call. Wait until you assess all of the first round of venues as the last thing you want to be doing is visiting too many venues.

2 Book the show around

Once you have whittled down your favourite venues based on their website information, reviews online, your phone call with them; you should then follow up with a phone call to that same coordinator and then schedule an appointment.

From that point and until you visit, you should have a notebook or use a notepad on your phone and compile questions. There are no stupid questions. Most wedding couples are in the same boat as you. Wedding coordinators are paid to give you information and ensure that you have all of the information that you need.

3 Visit

When you arrive, I recommend that you arrive early and go for a walk around before making yourself known to reception. Check out the service in the bar, restaurant and one of my pet peeves, check out the cleanliness of the toilets. Wedding days are very busy so it's important that standards don't slip when a venue is busy! You may build up more questions from your walk through.

4 Function room considerations

When you are looking at a function room, it is important to be able to visualize the room as it would appear on your wedding day. For most venues, they wouldn't have the venue set up for a wedding unless there was a wedding on the following day or that day. A lot of venues host Open Viewings whereby you can see the room set as it would be on your wedding day.

When you are looking at it dressed:

* Take a look at the linen – is it creased, are there stains?
* What is the lighting like in the room?
* Will you need to add some lighting such as uplighters, light up dance floor or fairy light backdrop?
* Is the bar inside the room? If it is outside the room, your guests may congregate around the bar. This could result in your wedding party being broken up. How big is the bar?
* Where are the wedding guest toilets? Are there separate toilets for wedding guests?
* What is the flooring like – is it tired and worn?
* Does every light fitting have a working light bulb? If not up to standard, your photos will need to be photo-shopped by your photographer.
* Is there wheel chair access?
* Where is the kitchen?
* Look up! Are there cob webs?
* Is there a stage for the band or do they set up on floor level?
* What décor is included?
* Will you need to bring in suppliers?
* Are there fresh flowers?
* Is there a PA system for speeches?
* What is the capacity of the room and what is the 'afters' capacity?

- Does the room have to be changed after the meal, where do guests go?
- What is the air conditioning or heat situation?
- Is there a cake table and stand?
- Where do you get your photographs taken?
- Is there any issue with you DIY'ing?
- Is there draping / fairy light backdrop or can you bring your own?

5 Pricing

Always get your coordinator to do a mock up bill based on your expected numbers and menu preference. Don't worry if this changes later on. This will give you a quick understanding of how much you can expect. Out of the quote you are given, find out about any extras that you could incur and what happens to price if your numbers go up or down.

Sample Wedding Venue Bill:

Here is a rough guide to pricing for your wedding. This list is not the same for every venue but it's an easy to use guideline. There has also been an emergence of 'All Inclusive Packages' which will have all of the essential items bundled. Most venues I know will expect you to prepay at least 48 hours before your big day.

1. Food

Cost for dinner per person. You may end up getting extra courses and supplement prices will apply. Don't forget to include yourselves in the numbers when calculating the bill!

2. **Wine**
   Estimate a half bottle per person. The split between red and white will depend on your menu but typically 50/50 is safe. A venue will always have overstock if you run out of either. You may decide to bring your own wine. In this case 'corkage' will apply. Check the rates for wine, sparkling and champagne as different prices may apply. Yes there is a charge to open a bottle of wine…..remember the venue has a business to run but always try and negotiate. The price of wine varies between venue but on average it is €20 per bottle. Therefore for it to be worth your while, you would need to be getting a good wine for apx €3/€4 per bottle. You will also have to store it, deliver it and if you are left with overstock, you will need to bring it home.

When you are being shown around, some of your questions may be answered so wait until the end of the visit to ask your outstanding questions. Most hotels conduct their show arounds in the sequence of how the day is run.

Tip

If you don't use all the pre-purchased wine, check if the venue will refund you. If they don't make sure to use your wine allocation. You could get them to keep the corks from all opened bottles and then count to make sure that you haven't been shafted!

3. **Toast Drink**
   You may end up doing a complimentary drink for everyone and you could estimate €6 per person, or alternatively you could do sparkling wine or champagne. There are 5 glasses per bottle so for a wedding of 100 guests = 20 bottles. Sparkling wine can start from €25 in some venues.

4. **Evening Finger Food/ The 'Afters'**
   You only need to cater for 50%-70% of the total number of guests in the room by evening time. This is usually served in between the band and DJ. It is always well received as after a few drinks who doesn't love some cocktail sausages and sandwiches! I wouldn't go too fancy on this- no one cares or notices so don't worry about canapés- the greasier the better!

5. **Bar Extension**

   Most venues are only licensed to serve until the standard bar closing times. Each venue is meant to apply for a late bar licence and the price they get depends on their solicitor fee's etc. Always see if this can be added complimentary as extra 2-3 hours of their bar tills ringing is in their interest!

6. **Arrival Food**

   Most venues supply the usual suspects- tea/coffee and biscuits. You may want to add some extras and there is a charge on this. Like evening food, there is no need to buy for everyone. 50%-60% is enough. Samples of arrival food include canapés, buns or sandwiches.

7. **Venue Hire**

   Not all venues charge for this. This is a flat fee or day hire rate for the exclusivity of the venue. Some charge 'minimum numbers' for key dates. This means that there may be a minimum requirement for your numbers to be 120 for a Saturday in September, if you have 80 people in your party, they may charge for 120 or put in a 'venue charge'.

Others say you must pay for several rooms. This means that your guests will pay for the rooms taking the pressure off you as a couple but beware, if your guests don't show up - you will have to pay.

Other types of charges

Other venues have other types of charges, make sure to ask what those charges are.

1. **Menu**

   When you book your wedding, don't get too bogged down in knowing what exact food you are going to have. You can confirm closer to the time and possibly when you know how much you can afford. Some items to ask include; can they cater for dietary requirements, how they charge for kids and what are the menu options, are there supplements for extra choices, have they won awards for food quality, will you get the opportunity to menu taste. It is also worth checking the provenance of the food, the more locally the food. Locally sourced food is better quality.

2. **Special touches**

   These are the personal extras that you want to add to create a unique feel to your wedding. You will need to ask what is included and what is their policy in you bringing in your own décor or small additions. If you are going to do your own décor, for example, dress the tables, will you need to come down the morning of the wedding and set up. Or will the venue dress the tables for you? If you want to bring in other suppliers to add in draping, dance floor or lighting for example, will they allow this? There can be issues with bringing in food vendors such as ice cream. The reason a venue may have an issue with external food vendors is traceability. If a member of your party gets food poisoning, the venue could be blamed instead of the vendor. All foods prepared at a venue will follow HACCP guidelines which should there be a need for investigation, will be ready to provide samples of food for inspection.

3. **Bar extensions**

   Some venues have to comply with the general bar closing

times that you would see your local pub adhering to. Most venues can offer a bar extension of up to 2 hours after general closing time. Some venues charge for this application.

4. **Insurance**

    All hotels and venues have to have public liability insurance. You cannot operate without it but if you are leasing a private venue, you may have to get your own personal liability. You should ask the venue what the policy is and what your liability is.

5. **Civil ceremony licence:**

    As discussed in the ceremony section, if you want to have a civil ceremony outside of the registry office and in your preferred hotel, you will need to check if the venue has been approved by the HSE. If it hasn't, you should ask them to push the approval process.

6. **Negotiating**

    When negotiating with your wedding coordinator, it is important that you don't fold and accept the very first offer. Some venues that are high demand will not budge. If you don't even ask, you could have done yourself out of a discount or some free add-ons without knowing. Always see if there is room to get a discount off the per head price. If that doesn't work, try and get some added extras thrown in. These added extras could be a champagne arrival for your guests or accommodation for your bridal party and parents.

7. **Minimum Numbers**

    Some venues have minimum numbers for key dates. This means that you have to have a minimum amount of guests to hold your wedding on that date. If your numbers fall short, you may be asked to pay a fee.

Contract

If you are happy with everything once you go through everything, you may decide to book the venue. At this point you will be given a contract to sign.

Wedding venue contracts are pretty standard. The following are the most common items you will find:

1. You can hold a date provisionally for 2 weeks before the deposit is due.

2. The deposit you pay will be non-refundable and transferable.

3. You will be required to pay the full bill before your wedding takes place.

4. If there is any damage caused by your guests, you might be liable for damage costs.

5. Some venues look for a second deposit a few months before the wedding.

6. A certain allocation of bedrooms will be allocated to you. Some venues may ask that if the rooms are not filled that the bride and groom pay the fees. This is considered part of the venue hire for some venues.

7. Your menu needs to be confirmed 2 weeks prior to your wedding date.

8. Prices are valid for a year from your booking date. Some venues prices change. Make sure that you are locking in your price.

9. Your bar extension will be marked here.

10. The hotel reserves the right to cancel your wedding should they feel it has been booked under false pretences, could harm the reputation of the venue or compromise the staffs safety.

11. The hotel also reserves the right to cancel your wedding in the event of unforeseen circumstances beyond their control; i.e. flood or fire for example.

12. No food or beverages are permitted to be brought on to the premises without discussion and agreement with venue. Your cake will be fine but this relates to alcohol and other food vendors. If you are bringing alcohol on site, they will impose a corkage fee and you will need to negotiate this fee. There is generally no problem if you are using the mini liquor bottles as favours.

13. The venue is not liable for the damage or loss of personal belongings.

Funding

Now that you have established how much the venue is going to be, you will have a good idea of how much you will need to save. The venue takes up the majority of your budget. In Ireland, a wedding budget can be anything from €10,000 to €40,000. This is a lot of money to try and save in one year.

When you start to book your wedding suppliers, you will need to pay deposits. A venue is usually €1000 and then each vendor after that is roughly €100 - €500. You can see that before you get in to really paying for your wedding, your initial deposit costs can be quite high.

When you start to think about budget, the core funding will come from the following:

✳ **Savings**
You may have some savings already in the bank and well done if you do. You may be starting out to save. If you are planning on saving for your wedding, you will need to know your end goal. Start saving a figure that will get you there at least a month before your wedding as that is when a lot of final payments are due. Banks offer fixed term savings accounts with interest rates so you could make your savings work a bit harder for you. Bonkers.ie allows you to compare savings rates. One thing to bear in mind is that some savings deals won't let you draw down any funds until a certain date. If you think you'll need funds to release during your planning stages, you should avoid accounts of this nature.

✳ **Parents**
This is now something that lives in the past. Gone are the days where parents pay for the full wedding. Parents may give you a cash gift to help you out with your wedding day. I always recommend not putting pressure on your parents as they may not be in a position to help and may feel very mixed emotions

with your wedding. They are excited that you are getting married but may be anxious as to how they will be able to financially support you.

✳ Bank / Credit Union loan

A very popular option is getting a loan. One thing to remember is that you have to pay it back! Most rates are from apx 9% APR. You can compare rates on Bonkers.ie. Some banks let you differ your repayments for up to 3 months so you could start to repay after your wedding.

Example of how much a loan may cost you

Loan Amount	€7,000
Rate	8.5% APR
Term of Loan	5 years
Per Month Re-payment	€142.62
Total Cost of Credit	**€1557.20**

Ref: Bank of Ireland January 2018. Lending rate 8.5% APR.

✳ Credit Card

The good thing about paying with credit card is that if there is a problem with the supplier, you can cancel the payment within a specific time frame. Credit Card costs can vary between providers and in general, the cost of credit could be anything from 10% to 30% of the debt you have clocked up. It is also very easy to lose the run of yourself with a credit card. It is ideal for your online shopping.

Chapter Three

Photographer

A photographer booking is date sensitive like your reception venue and ceremony. Therefore, you will need to book a photographer in good time to get your date. Good photographers book up fast.

H
ere are some considerations when booking your photographer.

Look at their work.

If you can meet at their studio or if they are exhibiting at a wedding fair, go and see them. It is better to meet them and chat through your ambitions. You should also look at their albums of previous work.

I am a firm believer that when you are booking a photographer, you are not just booking the physical photography, you are booking the person. It is important that you have a good relationship with your photographer as you want someone to bring the best out of you both on your wedding day. You also want a personality type that listens to what you want and your concerns. It is completely normal to dread pictures as it is way out of most peoples' comfort zones, a good photographer that you have a rapport with will put you at ease and ensure that you are comfortable.

Every photographer has a different style and humour. If you have a photographer that you just don't get, their humour on the day could feel antagonising whereas with someone else, they could be in stitches laughing.

Here are some questions to ask:

1. **Availability**
   Firstly, do they have your date and secondly, do they have anything else booked on the day. I recommend choosing a photographer that only has one event. If your photography runs over, you don't want them running out to another event.

2. **Reputation**
   You should ask how long they have been in business and

where you can review testimonials and real wedding features. Your photographer should have a good portfolio of weddings, you don't want your wedding to be their first run. It might be good to also ask if they have an assistant as you may not realise that a lot of photographers bring an extra shooter. When this person arrives at your house, you may think that the photographer has outsourced!

A photographer can only be in one place at one time. On the morning when couples leave from two different locations, they may need the help.

3. **Style**

What is their style? Ask them to describe it. More than likely it will be their style that has attracted you to them. Some photographers are very traditional whilst others could be more contemporary.

4. **Venue**

Are they familiar with the

venue that you have booked. If they are not, will they be doing a site visit before the day. You don't want to be winging it on the day. It is important that the photographer knows the nice spots and how lighting effects those spots. You could have a really beautiful setting but if the time of day lighting affects the photography outcome, it will be wasted.

5. **Run of the day**
Ask for a breakdown of timings of the day. You will need to know when they are arriving and leaving. Many photographers don't stay beyond the meal so if you want your speeches shot, you need to be specific and ask. An additional fee could be incurred. You should ask for a rough guide of shots that will be taken on the day.
Allow for this plan to be loose as on the day anything can happen and you should allow the creativity to flow from your photographer.

6. **Plan B**
You should have a plan for good weather versus bad weather! Also, do they bring extra equipment in case one camera fails!

7. **Price**
You need to agree your costings before you pay a deposit. Photographers can cost anything from €800 to €5000 with the main average being €1800. You will need to find out what is included within that price. For the mentioned prices you should have your days shoot up until meal, disc with images and album. Albums come in all shapes and sizes. The more elaborate the

" ...you want someone to bring the best out of you on your wedding day."

album, the more work the photographer needs to put in and hence why it would cost more. Do they charge extra for travel? Do they include an engagement shoot within your package?

8. **Production**

   Once your wedding is complete, how long will it be before your pictures are with you to review? What is involved with touch ups? Also check if there are additional charges for touch ups. Once you select your pictures for the album, how long will the album production and delivery take?

9. **Contract**

   You will be issued a booking form when you decide to go ahead. At this point you will need to sign and pay a deposit. The contracts are standard enough but be sure to read every item and if there is anything that you are unsure of, be sure to ask.

10. **Payment**

    What is the payment schedule? Is there a deposit to secure the date? Is that non-refundable and non-transferable? Do you have to pay in instalments and do you have to pre-pay in advance or is the remaining balance due after receipt of the final album. Be sure to find out about the refund or cancellation policy. It should be listed within the contract.

11. **Insurance**

    Most photographers are covered but you should ask the question to ensure that they have their own liability insurance.

12. **After – Usage**

    If you don't want your wedding pictures out there in public, you will need to advise your photographer as they may use some shots promotionally.

Chapter Four

Videographer

I have to say, I loved my wedding video and I probably watched this more than looking at my photos. It really captured the life of the wedding day.

always said that I wouldn't waste my money on a videographer for my wedding. I ended up booking one in the end as someone mentioned that it was lovely to look back at the speeches. I have to say, I loved my wedding video and I probably watched this more than looking at my photos. It really captured the life of the wedding day. You miss so much on the day. The day in itself can be a blur. When you watch the video, you get to see how the day went for your guests and what was going on while you were getting your pictures taken.

In terms of booking a videographer, the guide for booking a photographer is also very relevant. In addition, there are a items to consider.

1. **Their previous work**
   There is no better way to test your videographer than by just looking at their work. Most videographers have links on their website to their work.

2. **Style**
   Documentary, cinematic or perhaps a blend of both. What is your vision?

3. **Personality**
   Do they get you and understand what styles you like and what your vision is going to be?

4. **Locations**
   Do they travel to your destination. Do they know your location? Similar to the photographer, if they don't know the location, they may only be discovering it on the day. This will eat in to your time. Generally, your videographer will follow the lead of your photographer so it might be OK if they are not 100% familiar.

5. **Drones**
   A very popular piece of equipment is to have a drone. A drone is a camera that flies! Not every videographer has this equipment nor is it essential, but if you have seen footage of this effect, you should talk this through with your videographer.

6. Insurance
Do they have public liability insurance?

7. Equipment
Do you need to wear a mic during the ceremony and speeches. If you want to capture your vows in your video, you may need to have a microphone clipped on to you.

8. Second shooter
Do they need a second videographer with them to capture additional footage.

9. Booking
What do you need to do to secure the date? Do you need to pay a deposit and sign a contract?

10. Other events
Do they take on other jobs on the day of your wedding?

11. Coverage
You will also need to find out what is actually covered. Generally, the getting ready in the house right through to first dance is covered.

12. Usage
Once you have your finished product, videographers may use a show reel from your wedding to show case their work. If you are not comfortable with this, you will need to say it upon booking as it may be included in your contract.

13. How long have they been filming
It is always good to find out how long they have been filming weddings. There are some excellent videographers out there but they may not be familiar with weddings.

14. Contract
When it gets to the booking stage, you will be issued a contract to sign, you should read through this as it could contain items that you may not be comfortable with. This could include how your video will be used for promotional purposes.

15. End Result
What is the end produce, is it a disc with the full day or short snippets from each part of the day.

16. Background music

Your videographer will put background music to your piece, they will more than likely ask you what you would like.

17. Timings

You should get an idea of the run of the day or the videographer may want your photographers run of the day. They may be following their lead.

Chapter Five

Music

When choosing music for your wedding, I urge everyone
to listen or go and see the musicians that they
are interested in booking.

When choosing music for your wedding, I urge everyone to listen or go and see the musicians that they are interested in booking. A lot of well-established musicians have YouTube channels where you can listen to their music and see how they perform. Alternatively, you can always get a schedule of their upcoming appearances and go and see them.

There are several events throughout your day that require music.

1 Ceremony music

Whether you are getting married in a church or having a non-religious ceremony, you generally have music to walk up the aisle, music during the ceremony and music as you walk down the aisle.

The usual order of music during a ceremony is as follows:

1. **Pre-music**
   This is as the guests wait at your ceremony. It is background music and tends to be instrumental.

2. **Processional music**
   This is the music performed as the bridal party walks up the aisle.

3. **Ceremony music**
   While you light your candle, sign the registry and in a church have holy communion, you would have music during these stages. Your priest or celebrant will guide you to the times that music should be performed and your selected musicians will know too.

4. **End of ceremony music**
   As you walk out of the ceremony, there is a final song.

Some may do an extra song until everyone has left the church or registry.

2 Reception music

As your guests arrive at your venue, you could have some musical entertainment. It is generally understated background music which still allows guests to mingle.

Popular choices tend to be a solo pianist, harpist, string quartet or vocal harmony group.

 During the meal

Nine out of ten times your venue will pipe music through the background so that it's subtle. Some couples prefer to give a playlist on an iPod. Other couples prefer to have no music in the background at all. There is no protocol of what you should have.

Some couples add some entertainment through live music. There are bands that walk around the room playing instruments and singing.

Similar to the arrival reception music, some opt for soloists to add some ambiance to the room.

 Band

This can be one of the hardest things to pick as a couple. When it comes to a wedding band, there are so many. They come in various shapes and sizes. When you start to pick

a band, you are so conscious of pleasing your guests and having a full dancefloor.

A wedding band can cost anything from €800 to €3000. It all depends on what you are looking for. Prices are generally reflective of the level of experience and demand of the band.

There are various types of bands for you to choose from. You could pick a band that focuses on a particular genre. I had a 90's band and the dance floor was packed. I have been at weddings where an 80's band performed and again, dance floor packed. It all really depends on the crowd and your particular taste.

There are some bands that are very focused on wedding audiences. They cover as many aspects to cater for the diverse range of guests.

Regardless of the type of band you choose, if you are going to be spending the money that is required you must go and see them. There is no issue dropping in to someone else's wedding to see the band perform. You should also read reviews across wedding forums. You may have attended a wedding and saw a band that you loved, which is even better!

When booking your band, you will sign a contract and have to pay a deposit. The deposit tends to be 10% of the total cost although some bands may have different requirements. You should read the contract and ensure that you understand all aspects. Some bands stipulate that they are to be provided with some snacks and water. You should ask your venue to keep some afters food aside for them and to have a jug of water ready. Most bands play for two to two and half hours.

You will also agree on a set list when you book. If there are particular songs that you love or hate, make this known to the band.

You would also discuss your first dance song at this stage. For some couples, they have a 'song' but for others, this can be the hardest thing to pick. Some couples also opt to learn a dance routine. If you are going to do this, make sure that your band knows the exact version that you are rehearsing to. They may have a special way of performing that song and different beats could put you off. Some don't have the band perform their first dance and instead play the song from the actual artist.

It would also be worth checking what space they

need in your venue or if they are familiar with your venue. Make sure to make note of the time that they arrive and set up.

The DJ follows on after the band. How long your DJ plays until is generally in line with your bar extension. If you haven't got a bar extension, normal bar close times apply and your DJ would follow suit. In most cases, they play for two to three hours.

If you can go and see the DJ that would be good. For many but it's not as essential as going and seeing a band. A lot of bands provide a DJ and it can be more cost effective to go with that option.

You should also check what time they arrive at and set up. It is worth checking if they bring equipment as some like to bring lighting.

Most wedding DJ's require a deposit to secure the date but a lot are OK with full payment on the night. Typical DJ costings are from €250 to €600. It is also advisable to keep some snacks and water aside for your DJ.

Band vs DJ

There are some couples that decide to not have a band and just have a DJ for the full night. There are no rules around this. It is cheaper to go with a DJ for the whole event, some prefer the disco feel and the non-restriction of music genres. Others prefer the experience of a live band. It is completely down to the couple.

Be your own DJ

I have heard that there is a growing number of couples opting to plug in their music device and flow through the venues' sound system. It gives the couple the option to play whatever they want. They create their own playlists and guests can be the DJ too. There is no cost involved here, just your time in creating a five-hour playlist. The only drawback here is that a DJ knows how to build up an atmosphere to get the party going. You will need to design your playlists to build up to the dance floor.

Chapter Six

Flowers

This is one of my favourite parts of wedding planning. Flowers are one of the main ways to set the tone for your wedding day. Flowers can represent various themes and can be a subtle or as extravagant as your budget allows.

The first item on the agenda is to decide if you will book a florist or if you will do your own flowers. If you do not have any experience in floral arranging, I would advise letting the professional look after you. I have seen so many DIY disasters! There is a big misconception that floristry is easy. It is quite technical and you will need to know your stuff if you plan on doing your bouquets or church arrangements. I tend to find it easier to DIY your table centrepieces (within reason).

Choosing your florist

Before you start hunting for a florist, I recommend going to Pinterest to get an idea of styles that you like. You can search for wedding flower boards and you will get so much inspiration. You should pin the pictures to a secret board and bring them to your appointment.

It can be hard to find florists as a lot of them don't have websites and don't advertise. You tend to find that most are booked through word of mouth. The first place to start is by asking your venue to recommend or to check out their recommended supplier list. By getting a florist recommended by the venue, you can be sure that the florist knows what works best.

Tip: You should always be mindful not to go with highly scented flowers. This can drive guests with hay fever mad.

You can also visit the Wedding Florist section on IrishWeddingBlog.ie for recommendations.

Once you find a florist you like, you will need to discuss flower types that you like and what is within budget. If the florist has a lot of experience with weddings, they will more than likely have some samples of previous work. This might make it easier for you to choose.

What to consider

There are various factors that should be considered when choosing your wedding flowers:

1. **Time of year**
   To keep your costs down, you should always try and go with the flowers that are in season. Your florist will advise you on what will work best.

2. **Venue style**
   Your venue may already provide some flowers. Your venue will also have a style that you want to work with.

3. **Your style**
   There are certain flowers that match different styles. Your florist will be able to advise, plus your Pinterest board should be able to get this across.

4. **Colour of bridal party dresses / overall colour scheme**
   You may want to coordinate your flowers with the overall colour scheme of the wedding. Some opt to keep flowers neutral but you can also add splashes of colours within your arrangements.

5. **Budget**
   You may have a figure in mind and that will determine the type of flower you go for and how many of that flower you will get.

6. **Logistics & storage**
   Will your flowers be delivered the morning of or night before? You will need a storage solution. After the ceremony, you may want to bring some of the flowers to the venue. Appoint someone to do this for you.

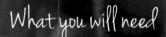

What you will need

* Bouquet for bride
* Button holes for bridal party
* Bridesmaid bouquets
* Flower girl bouquets
* Floral spray for candle
* Church / ceremony pedestals
* Pew ends
* Bouquets as gifts for mothers and grand mothers
* Some opt for venue flowers

Chapter Seven

Beauty

A brides' beauty regime in the lead up to their wedding day can be pretty full on. For some, this can be a year long preparation. Some engage in laser therapy for hair removal and skin improvements. Whilst others hit the gym.

For this part of the book, the focus will be on hair and make up for the actual wedding day.

Hair

When you start to search for your hair dresser, there should be a few things to keep in mind.

1. Do you want them to travel to your house or venue that you plan to leave from?

2. Will you need to travel to them?

3. Do they specialise in wedding hair? Up-styling is very different from colouring. Not all hair dressers specialise in this area. You will need to book someone that understands weddings as the time frames, equipment needed etc, are different from a normal day at the office! A bride will also want a more involved service and the stylist should understand this too.

When you find your stylist, here are your to-do items:

* **Trial**
  Book your trial for a time that suits you both. If you are hoping to get an up-style, you should wash and dry your hair the night before.

* **During Your Trial**
  Bring some of the images that you have collected so that the stylist can get an idea of what you are looking for. It is also a good idea to bring a picture of the dress and accessories. This way they can create a look that will complement the overall style.

* **Cut regularly**
  You will be advised to try and get your hair to the healthiest version and most stylists will recommend that you get your hair trimmed and get a treatment regularly in the lead up to the big day.

* **Don't get anything majorly new**
  Most advise you to stay away from doing anything radically new before the big day.

Time of year

This is not overly important but if there is a style that isn't wind friendly and you are planning a winter wedding, you should probably reconsider!

Type of hair

Your length, style, texture and volume will be factors to consider when choosing what style will work best for you. A good hair stylist will be able to advise you as to what would work best for you.

Bridesmaids and other bridal party

When you are budget planning, you will need to factor in your bridesmaids' hair. Some also request that both mothers and flower girls' hair is done by the stylist. You may need a second stylist pending number of heads that need to be done.

Timing on the day

I recommend getting your hair stylist to put the run of the day in writing for you. Your photographer and make-up artist may run their schedules around your hair timings.

Make Up

Getting your make-up done can immediately transform you and make you feel like a million dollars. The day of your wedding is no different. Before your big day, it is important that you select the right make-up artist (MUA) for you.

To find the right MUA, it is important to do your homework. I recommend that you look for recommendations from previous brides and most importantly, look at the MUA's work.

Once you short list your favourite artists, you should book a trial. Most MUA's charge for the trial. You could pay anything from €30 to €50 per trial.

Trial Tips

✳ In advance of your trial, start collecting images of looks that you like. You can bring these images with you. You can work through them with your MUA at the start of the trial.

✳ Your MUA will be able to advise you on best looks for your face shape, features and colouring.

✳ It is very important to select a professional MUA as they will know what techniques and products work best for photography. The camera highlights everything so it is important that the right stuff is being used. A professional MUA will have either an ITEC/NVQ qualification or have worked with one of the leading make up brands for several years.

✳ You should bring images of your dress and accessories and give an indication of what style your hair will be.

✳ During the trial, your MUA should be making note of what products are being used and any special requirements.

✳ There's no such thing as a stupid question. I always encourage brides to ask as many questions about the application and products during the trial.

* Your MUA should give you skin care advise which you should apply in the lead up to your wedding.

* When you see the result, if you are not happy, call it. Don't suffer in silence. The MUA wants to make you happy so it is important that you are happy.

* Discuss prices. You should get a written quote and make sure that you are aware of all costs per head and travel.

* You should get an idea of timings on the day. Keep this for your photographer and videographer.

* It takes an average of 40-45 minutes per application. Your trial should take an hour and a half. If you have more than 4/5 people to get their make-up done, you may need a second artist. Your MUA may have someone that they work with and can bring them with them on the day.

Chapter Eight

The Dress

This is one of the most exciting, emotional and daunting parts of planning your wedding. It can be overwhelming pressure to find the perfect dress.

There are so many styles and trends change every season. This means that there is almost too much choice. You can spend anything from €500 to €20,000 upwards. Weddingsonline.ie cite the average spend on a wedding dress is €1600.

Where to start

1. Start to collect pictures of the dresses that you like. You will see images on social media, Pinterest, Instagram, blogs and magazines. Once you start collecting, you will start to see style trends emerging. That will be a starting point for you.

2. It is advised to shop for your dress 6-8 months in advance of your wedding. I prefer to air on the side of caution and shop a year in advance.

3. If there is a dress you like, you may decide to try it on. You will need to see what bridal shops stock it. You should phone and ask if they stock that dress.

4. If it is a bridal store that you choose to buy from, you will need to book an appointment.

5. Weekends are very busy appointment days. Try to book a mid-week appointment as you won't feel as pressured.

When it comes to shopping for a dress, there are many places that you can choose from.

Where to Buy

✳ **Bridal Stores**
This is the most popular way that brides to be shop.

✳ **Bespoke designer**
For some brides, they want something unique and tailored. The turnaround time for a bespoke gown varies but 10 months appears to be the average.

✳ **Pre-loved / Second Hand Shops**
Sites like Donedeal allows brides to buy and sell used wedding dresses. Charity shops also stock a range of pre-loved as well as stock that did not sell from other stores.

* **Online**
  There are many online shops that you can buy wedding dresses from across the world. I advise that you only buy from a reputable seller than has a return policy.
* **Rental Stores**
  If you don't want to make a large investment, this is a great alternative.
* **Bridal Outlets**
  Outlets offer heavily discounted gowns which are generally from last season.
* **Trunk Shows**
  Most bridal stores cannot carry a designers' full range. This can be down to cost or size of boutique. On some occasions, the designer may come to the boutique or another venue and bring their full collection.
* **Wedding Fairs**
  A wedding fair is a fantastic opportunity for you to meet various bridal stores. The large-scale wedding shows are the best for this. They will bring their feature gowns

and will also appear in a fashion show. You can

It is advised to shop for your dress 6-8 months in advance of your wedding.

book an appointment at these shows. Some allow you try on dresses and you can even buy.

* **Sample Sale**
  Most bridal stores have a sample rail but there are pop up shops that can appear with a huge range of samples. If you have ever seen the Friends episode when Monica is buying her dress…..well this is what a sample sale is like.

The Appointment

Before you start to get stuck in to trying on dresses, it is very important that you let them know your maximum budget. Some shops will always chance their arm by bringing you dresses that are a few hundred over your budget. Be very straight with your budget and ask them not to show dresses over your stated budget.

A good sales person will be able to tell you what is the right style for your shape. You may have a preference of style and you can communicate this to your sales advisor. Keep an open mind as sometimes, it's the dress that you least expect that looks the best on you! The sales advisor will start the process by establishing what dress styles you like.

Dress Types

Ball Gown	Suits most figure types
A-Line	Suits most figure types
Trumpet	Stunning on hour glass shapes
Mermaid	Beautiful on hour glass and if you have broad shoulders
Sheath	Beautiful on hour glass type figures
Empire	Very flattering on non-curvy, athletic and straighter figures
Tea Length	Suits most figures but ideal for those with height
Mini	Works well for petite frames
Alternative	The beauty of an alternative style is you work with your personality. Some choices include bridal jump suits, suits and non-bridal dresses

When you find the style that suits, the dress may come in various colours and materials.

Colours

* White
* Ivory
* Champagne
* Blush
* Floral
* Pastel hues

Some dresses have one piece of material with additional embellishments. Others have layers and have a few different types of materials.

Materials

* Silk
* Lace
* Taffeta (slight sheen)
* Satin
* Georgette
* Dupioni
* Organza
* Chiffon
* Tulle
* Charmeuse

Some dresses have a type of train. There are names for the different lengths. Brush is the shortest, Court is the next, Chapel is the length where you start to see a distinctive train. Chapel always comes with a hook up, Cathedral is my favourite and is 6ft in length. Royal is the longest and is 10ft long. There is a 'watteau' which starts from the shoulders of the dress rather than within the skirt.

When you find the perfect dress. You will probably start to accessorize. Most boutiques will have matching veils, hair clips, shoes, dress accessories, bags and jewellery.

Top Tips

- If you plan on wearing heels on your big day, make sure to bring a pair with you so that you get a true sense of how the dress will sit on you.
- Allow 1-1.5 hours for your appointment.
- Keep your entourage small. Too many opinions can be overwhelming.
- Bring an adjustable bra. Some dresses are strapless, backless, one shouldered amongst many more. If you have bought specific underwear for your big day, bring it with you.
- You should ask if they will do your alterations. Some have a seamstress contracted to their store. It's best to go with their seamstress as if anything goes wrong, the shop will accept the liability. It is generally cheaper to go with an external seamstress.
- The store should give you a timeframe of delivery in writing. Dresses take roughly 6 months to arrive in store. You will then need to allow for alterations time.
- Every store works back from your wedding date. Give the store a few weeks before your wedding date just in case. I ran in to trouble with a late delivery for my dress and it was incredibly stressful.
- Make sure to find out if there are any hidden costs.
- Most bridal boutiques have a sample rail with last season's dresses. These are the dresses that were just tried on. They are generally in fantastic condition. They are heavily discounted. It is worth a look!

Chapter Nine

Bridesmaids

When I went to shop for bridesmaid dresses with my bridesmaids, we were in and out within 45 minutes....now this is not the norm!

The rule of thumb is to get the dresses 6 months before the big day. I preferred to shop earlier as the colour of the dresses was going to dictate the colour of my flowers and stationery. This is not that important to everyone but it was just something that I wanted to get off my to-do list!

In terms of budget, you can spend anything from €30 to €500 per dress. It depends on where and how you buy.

I get asked 'what should a bride pay for' when it comes to bridesmaids. If you have asked someone to be your bridesmaid, it is customary that you provide the dress and shoes. If there is a shawl required, that would also be expected to be purchased by the bride.

Where to Buy

1. **Online**

    I find that more and more brides are shopping online for the bridesmaid dresses. I have seen disastrous dresses bought online. They were nothing like the pictures online. There are a few sites that are highly reputable and the best way to know this is by looking at their reviews, return policy and what is on their social media sites.

    Dessy is good and most bridal shops stock that range. You can get every possible colour under the sun as well as every style variation. They also have a section to match accessories. There is a grooms wear accessory section and you can get ties, pocket squares and much more in the same colour scheme as the bridesmaid dresses. ASOS is very popular, it has very reasonably priced dresses and a quick delivery and return policy. If you are buying online, there are measurement guidelines on most reputable sites. They give you the size guide based on their actual measurements. It is important that your bridesmaids give you their exact measurements.

2. **High Street**

   So many high-street retailers have formal wear lines and they are generally very reasonably priced. You don't need an appointment; you can pop in and try on at any stage.

3. **Bridal Store**

   A lot of bridal stores stock bridesmaid dresses and some are solely dedicated to bridesmaids. The process is the same as buying a wedding dress. You will need an appointment and you will get a dedicated service.

   If you are hitting the high street or a bridal store; you should have an idea of what you would like in advance. You should discuss this with your bridesmaids before you enter the store. Otherwise you could end up with time wasting. The important thing is to stay focused as there will be a lot of opinions and ideas. This is also where conflict within bridal parties can start.

4. **Pre-Loved**

   If you are lucky, you may be able to get your dresses in one of the pre-loved/second hand boutiques. Alternatively, there are buy and sell sites that might have some dresses. You could save yourself a lot of money.

5. **Rental**

   I am hearing of more and more bridal parties opting to rent the dresses rather than buying. It is a fantastic idea! I don't know many that wear their bridesmaid dresses after the wedding!

Dresses

✳ You will need to decide if you want a full length or short dress. It is important to be mindful of your bridesmaid preferences, particularly with short dresses as not everyone wants to have their legs out.

✳ Adjustable dresses are a brilliant choice as they allow for many different shapes and sizes. If you have a pregnant bridesmaid, this is the type of dress you want.

✳ There used to be extreme pressure for one style to fit all. Luckily, the trend has shifted to allow mismatched styles and colours so that your bridesmaids can be more comfortable.

✳ Jumpsuits are becoming increasingly popular. This is a trend and like all trends, they will go out of fashion in time.

Chapter Ten

Suits

It is customary to wait until the bride and bridesmaid dresses have been picked. Suit shopping generally takes place 4-6 months in advance.

I t is customary to wait until the bride and bridesmaid dresses have been picked. Suit shopping generally takes place 4-6 months in advance.

The process of getting the suit tends to be a much simpler process in comparison to other wedding planning activities.

Most suit shops are happy for the groomsmen and fathers to come in at different times to the groom. An appointment should be booked for each visit. Generally, the groom and either best man or father of the groom visit the store. A lot of brides go to the initial suit selection visit. They will select the suits and then the remaining party can come in at another stage to get measured.

If you are buying suits from the high street, you would probably need everyone together to ensure that you are getting all the right pieces together.

If you have flexibility to shop during the week rather than the weekend, I highly recommend that you do this. You will feel less pressured and will have the full attention of the sales person.

Before you hit the shops, it is important to have an idea of colour. Suit colours can include; Navy, Black, Blue, Tweed, Charcoal, Grey, Brown, White and Pastels.

Where to source your suits

* **Suit Hire Shop (rent)**
  If you are looking for nothing out of the ordinary then renting is perfect. Footwear can also be rented. If renting, make note of collection and return times. You should also enquire about penalties for being late or if the suits are soiled. Allow one hour for your first appointment.

* **Tailors**
  Some grooms opt to get their suit created from scratch. This may not be provided for the rest of the bridal party. The groom would meet with the tailor to give an idea of the type of suit they want designed and made. It can take anything from 3-5 months for the suit to be completely ready. It depends on the tailors' availability.

* **Suit Shop (buy)**
  You could hit the high street and get suits in any of the menswear retailers. This can be a good idea if you want the bridal party to keep their suits after the wedding.

> **Tip**
> When you are trying on your suit do a squat or crouch down – if the trousers do not split then they won't split on the dance floor!

To customize your wedding look and to bring colour and individuality you can achieve this through accessories such as socks, shoes, laces, runners rather than shoes, suspenders, pocket squares, tie, bow ties, button holes (flowers) and belts. Different members of the male party can have different features to distinguish their role. For example, both fathers could have a different type of tie or waist coat.

Type of suits

✴ **Morning Suit**
This is the classic and most popular wedding suit. A morning suit consists of a tail coat which can be single or double breasted, a dress shirt, waist coat and trousers. A tie, cravat or bow tie can be worn. Most grooms would rent this type of suit as it's not something that he would get multiple wears out of.

✴ **Tuxedo**
The Tux is for a black-tie wedding. It consists of a single-breasted jacket, dress shirt and dickie bow/bow tie. Some wear a waist coat too. This is a popular rental but a lot buy as there is opportunity for post wear.

✴ **Lounge Suit**
This is the most informal and most will buy rather than rent. There is a lot of post wear opportunity with this type. This is a nice slim fit or general 2-piece suit. Some add a waist coat for the occasion of the wedding to make it more formal.

✴ **Uniform**
If your groom works in the military, there is the option to wear this uniform.

Chapter Eleven

Transport

A wedding car can cost anything from €300 upwards. You will need to decide how many cars you want. It is advisable to book your car at least 6 months in advance of your wedding date.

Most couples will book 2 cars. 1 that will bring the groom from his location and then come back for bridesmaids. The second car is for the bride and will end up bringing both bride and groom to the venue after the ceremony.

Some couples provide a bus for guests. This is becoming less of an expectation.

The type of transport you go for will probably depend on the overall style of your wedding day. You could go for a vintage, modern or quirky car.

Quirky or novelty ideas include;

* Tractors
* Racing Cars
* Ice Cream Van
* Vintage Camper Van
* and I recently spotted a Garda car!

A horse and carriage is also an option. It is not as popular as it used to be and may only be viable where the ceremony location is close to the venue or house the bride leaves from.

Whatever car type you choose, think about your dress and will you be able to get in and out with ease.

Booking

I recommend going to one of the wedding shows as you will get to see a few different vendors under one roof. It saves a lot of hassle. A lot of the car suppliers at the wedding shows tend to offer a discount if you book on the day.

* Before you commit to paying a deposit, look for reviews on wedding forums and social media.

* Get your vendor to put all inclusions in writing.

* Some charge mileage as well as rental for the vehicle. Make sure you know of all hidden costs.

* Get the timings of the day in writing.

* Most vendors will include champagne and your choice of music.

* Ask what the plan b is if anything happens to the car you have booked. Vintage cars are prone to issues.

* Will they provide ribbon?

* Will there be any other bookings on the day and will this affect your timings?

Tip
If you are trying to save on budget. A good place to start is by looking for someone you know with a fancy car.

It is important that you gather all the above information before signing the contract. Read the contract and ask for clarity if anything is unclear.

Chapter Twelve

Stationery

Your wedding stationery is the key to setting the tone
to your wedding day.

O nce you have your colour scheme and overall theme of your wedding decided, you could start to look at your stationery. Be very careful at this stage as this is where a lot of couples tend to go over budget.

Your stationery will include

- Save the date cards
- Invitation pack – send out 2 months before wedding. RSVP date is generally 3-4 weeks before the actual wedding day. You may have to write in names and addresses on the invites. Mistakes are common so just have some extras in case!

- Ceremony booklet
- Table Plan
- Table numbers (if not provided by venue)
- Guest place name card
- Menu (if not provided by venue)
- Thank you cards
- Signage

The Invitation Pack

Most invitation packs will include the actual invite with details of ceremony, reception, date and times. In support of this card, you would generally include details such as location of ceremony and reception, accommodation options and if there are plans for a second night of celebrations.

The final inclusion is the RSVP card with addressed envelope.
The RSVP will include a tick box for attendance or non-attendance as well as an area to let the couple know of any special requirements.

Tip — Don't forget to take the cost of postage in to account when budgeting.

As a rule of thumb, the heavier the paper weight and the more treated the paper is – the more expensive it is. Certain treatments such as engraving, embossing and use of metallic colours will push the cost.

Many couples opt for gold font for the invitations. Some gold and lighter colours can be difficult to read. The same applies to intricate calligraphy; if it is too fancy it can be illegible.

On your RSVP, include an email address and phone number. This allows guest to give their answer in a prompt manner.

It is customary to send out your invitations 2 months before the wedding with an RSVP date of 2-3 weeks before the actual date. My advice would be to send it out two and half months before and with an RSVP date of 5 weeks before the wedding. I spent a long time following up with invitees and it allows you to get your table plan finalised in good time. If you are inviting guests from abroad, you should their invites earlier to allow them enough notice to book flights.

Sourcing your stationery

* When you decide to source your stationery, the most cost effective way is to choose an existing set from a stationery provider. There are also pre-made templates online which you can print yourself. Generally, they don't turn out very well.

* If you want something unique, you could get a designer to create a bespoke look for your wedding. Etsy has a wealth of designers that are reasonably priced.

* It is possible to hire a calligraphist to write your invites for you. It can look beautiful but a luxury like this will depend on your budget.

* An emerging trend is sustainable wedding invitations. You can get some nice e-invites. You simply source an online template, upload your guest emails and the system manages the rest and the RSVP process. In saying that, as a guest, I love to have an invite in my hands. A sustainable alternative is the 'Seeded' wedding invitation. The paper is made from seeds which means that guests can plant your wedding invitation when they are ready to part with your wedding information.

Chapter Thirteen

Wedding Rings

Buying your wedding rings should be a lot easier than buying an engagement ring. It is advisable to shop 6 months before your wedding day.

You can buy your wedding rings in any high street or specialist jewellers. For a unique design, you would need the ring custom made and there are many great Irish designers available.

In the more traditional jewellers, they will give you a personalised wedding coin for free.

Here are some considerations when choosing your wedding rings:

* **Colour**
  You will have a choice of silver, gold, white gold, rose gold and platinum. Most couples will go with the colour of the engagement ring.

* **Shape**
  Some bands are rounded at the edges whilst others flat. If you have an engagement ring with a special feature, your wedding band may have a bend in it to cater for the engagement ring.

* **Stones**
  This is not essential but some couples choose a wedding ring with incrusted stones.

* **Engraving**
  Jewellers will offer engraving for the inside of the ring (space permitting). If you wanted some engraving work done on the outer part of the ring, it may need to be sent to a specialist designer.

* **Size**
  When trying on your ring, make note of the heat. If you are cold your finger is smaller and when hot it expands. Your rings should be comfortable in both circumstances.

Chapter Fourteen

The Cake

This is one the best parts about planning a wedding. Not only do you get to look at pretty cakes but you get to taste them too. You will probably want a cake that reflects the theme or style of your wedding. The cake assists in bringing the overall look together.

When choosing your cake, you only need to focus on 2 things – the taste and the look.

Most bakers will offer 2-6 tiers and some provide displays with a water feature. 3 tiers can cover up to 100 guests and 5 tiers up to 200 guests.

Many bakers allow different flavours per tier which is always a great hit. Traditionally, couples opted for a fruit top tier and kept it for the christening of their first-born. You can freeze the fruit layer. This tradition has fizzled out over the last few years.

When you select your baker, you will be invited to visit their bakery for a tasting. It is important to establish if the baker complies with HACCP. This is a hygiene standard for commercial kitchens. You can also taste some cake at a wedding fair. It is difficult to talk at the fairs and you may still need a follow-on appointment.

You will probably have an idea of the look of the cake you want but it is important to decide the flavours first.

Flavours

* Chocolate biscuit
* Red velvet
* Carrot cake
* Lemon drizzle
* Chocolate (Belgian is my favourite)
* Victoria sponge with raspberry and cream filling
* Vanilla
* Hazelnut especially when mixed with chocolate
* Peanut butter
* Nuts
* Coffee
* You can also do some boozy options; Grand Marnier is gorgeous mixed with chocolate.
* Fruit cake

Once you know flavours, you may want to select an icing.

Icing Options

* Buttercream
* Fondant
* Chocolate
* Sugar
* Marzipan

Now that you've picked tiers, flavour and icing; you will now need to select the style and decoration.

Decoration

Basic cakes have 3 tiers, white sugar icing and is dressed with ribbon or flowers.

More elaborate versions have very intricate sugar craft designs. The more detail you have, the more time the baker needs to spend which ultimately increases the price.

Naked cake has become very popular and is ideal for a rustic or whimsical style wedding.

You will also need to decide if you want a cake topper. A cake topper is the piece that you place at the very top of the cake. There are so many ideas out there and very easily sources through Etsy, Newbridge Silverware, wedding fairs, Amazon or you could make one yourself. There are specialized crafts people that can make novelty figurines.

Money saving tips

✳ Wedding cake prices start from €250 and can go up to €1500. To save on budget, Marks and Spencers sell wedding cake tiers and you can add your own special touches. Another way to keep the cost down is to dress your cake with flowers and fresh fruit.

✳ Some brides make their own cake or have a friend or family member that offers.

✳ You could also have a styrofoam cake which is a fake display cake. You could borrow a display piece from a baker.

✳ Rather than cutting cost, you could look to ensure that you get better value by doubling a slice of wedding cake in a box as a favour for guests.

✳ You could ask the venue if serving your wedding cake as a dessert is an option. The idea is that you remove the cost of dessert from your venue price. Some venues will do this and knock the price down whilst others stand firm on the price and still charge the full amount regardless. It is at the wedding venues discretion.

Alternatives to wedding cakes

✳ Cup cakes
✳ Jelly cake
✳ Cheese board
✳ Donut wall or donut tower cake
✳ Homemade dessert table
✳ Profiterole cake
✳ Macaroon cake
✳ Candy cart
✳ Wedding cake pops

✳ Truffle cake
✳ Pancake/crepe station
✳ Brownie wedding cake
✳ Ice cream cake or ice cream cones
✳ Cheese cakes
✳ Italian flan
✳ Chocolate fountain
✳ Waffle station

Finer details

The booking process of your cake is no different to booking most other items. You will need to pay a deposit and sign a contract. You should get your cake maker to confirm all cake details in the contract.

Ask them to make note of delivery times and final payment details in the contract. Most will deliver to the venue on the day and will set up for you. Others will ask you to collect and you may have to drop to the venue the night before.

If you must collect the cake you will need to have someone do this for you. It will need to be transported to the venue. Venues will take in the cake the night before and store it in their refrigerator or cold room. You could also ask the venue to set the cake on the display table.

A tip for transporting the cake – do not stack the boxes – put pillows around each box and if you have a large plastic tub, place one over each box.

Make sure to discuss your cake requirements with your wedding coordinator at the venue. If you wish to keep some of the cake you should let them know as some could end up throwing out what's left.

Chapter Fifteen

Honeymoon

By the time your honeymoon comes around, you will be ready for a break. Your honeymoon will be a trip of a lifetime probably the only time in your life where you will get a nice long break from work.

Your honeymoon should be booked 6-8 months prior to your wedding. I booked mine at about 10 months as Tour America hosted their annual 'Red Cow Sale'. We saved almost €1,000 on our honeymoon by booking at this event.

There is a large amount of research that needs to go in to planning a honeymoon. Not only will you have to find the destination you want but you will also have to decide on the hotel, activities, flights, tour operator and so much more. My time was very limited so I booked my honeymoon with a tour operator for ease. They planned everything and I just had to turn up! There is an assumption that it is more expensive to go with a tour operator/travel agent. In the case of my honeymoon to Orlando and Cancun, it worked out cheaper to book through a travel agent.

You will be investing a lot in this trip. It important to know that it is in safe hands. The average cost of a honeymoon for Irish couples is €4000.

Some larger travel agents offer a 'Honeymoon Registry'. Your guests can gift you towards your honeymoon.

The most popular honeymoon destinations include:

* USA
* Mexico
* South Africa
* Maldives
* Bora Bora
* Barbados
* Seychelles

* Dubai
* Thailand
* Caribbean
* Portugal
* Italy

Staying at home in Ireland is also very popular.

When deciding on honeymoon, you will both need to establish what you want. Some want a luxurious all-inclusive retreat or do you want an adventure?

Another consideration is when to travel. Will you jump on the plane the day after the wedding or wait for a few weeks?

Certain tropical destinations have rain seasons.

The more flexible you are on travel times, the better the deal you could avail of.

A good time to shop for a honeymoon is during the January sales. If you are flexible with your time, you could hold out for a last-minute cancellation and get your honeymoon at a heavily discounted rate.

Keep an eye out extra costs in the location that you will be travelling to. Some countries add a city and state tax which will add to your costs.

Bring a copy of your wedding invitation with you. If you present it at some resorts, they will upgrade you or add some bubbly to your room!

Make sure to book your trip in both names. If you haven't changed your married name on your passport, do not use your married name on your bookings.

Print out your itinerary and booking confirmation details just in case there are issues with your bookings.

Very Important!!

Check your passport expiry dates. If your passport expires during your honeymoon, you will need to get a new one. Allow 3-6 weeks for your passport.

If travelling to the USA, make sure that you have an ESTA or that your current one is valid.

It is advisable to have travel insurance for your trip.

Chapter Sixteen

Insurance

If you are getting married in an approved and insured venue, you can rest assured knowing that this responsibility is in the hands of the venue!

hosted my wedding in my husbands' grandmothers' back garden. This meant that it wasn't an approved commercial venue and had no commercial insurance. This would be the case for a lot of barn and marquee weddings. The main issue we faced was if someone fell or hurt themselves. This was one of the hardest things to source and we had to get Public Liability Insurance in our names. It was €200 and in my case, you couldn't put a price on peace of mind!

If you are getting married in an approved and insured venue, you can rest assured knowing that this responsibility is in the hands of the venue! If you are bringing in third parties – decorators, drapers or lighting, it is outside of the venues responsibility. You should ask all third parties for their insurance liability.

Tip

Wedding Insurance won't cover you if you change your mind. It is the safety blanket for those 'just in case' incidences that we all hope won't happen on our special day.

General wedding cover usually comprises of cover for a genuine issue whereby a supplier failed to show up or provide a service.

The cost is dictated by the level of cover you need. Cover starts at €35 and can go up to €250 pending on cover required.

If you have home or contents insurance, you should call your insurer and let them know if gifts, dresses, rings etc are now in the house. In some cases, your insurer may be able to add on a package for the period of your wedding to your policy which will cover you.

You should also invest in travel insurance for your honeymoon.

Chapter Seventeen

Décor & Extras

When you have finalised your stationery and flowers, you will now have the starting point of your colours and themes ready. Your wedding décor allows you to personalise your wedding day.

This is where most couples lose the run of their wedding budget. You will start to see so many novelties and must resist a lot of temptation.

Try to stay focused. You are at the very end of your budget and you have done so well up until this point!

Your wedding venue will have some décor and this may be enough. If your budget is tight, just work with what you have. You can build on the venue styling and not break the bank.

Some examples of décor and extras include;

- Ice cream carts
- Table centrepieces
- Candy carts
- Light up letters
- Light up dance floor
- Lighting in general
- Photo booth
- Table plan
- Chocolate fountain
- Champagne fountain
- Dance or another entertainment act
- Favours
- Food stations such as prosecco bar, crepe station, dessert tables…you name it

And this list doesn't even cover a tenth of what's out there!

Inspiration

You can draw inspiration from anywhere but some of the most popular destinations are;

1. Specialist companies such as Frog Prince Weddings, Wild Feather Events and Styling, Vintage Affair and so much more.

2. Online shops including Etsy, Favour Lane, Pearls and Lace. My Wedding Shop and Hen World.

3. Online 'Buy, Sell & Rent' sites or Facebook groups

4. Second hand shops and car boot sales

5. Raid your grandmother's house (that's what we did!)

6. Pinterest – suppliers post their stock here

7. IKEA – Every year I take over IKEA's event section and create a wedding wonderland showcasing how you can use IKEA's products to create a personalised and DIY wedding.

8. Other real weddings. You can tune in to Irish Wedding Blog or other wedding websites and draw inspiration from other couples wedding day style.

You can also visit the décor section of Irish Wedding Blog for up to date décor inspiration.

Chapter Eighteen

The Crisis

Ah you can't beat a good old crisis when it comes to a
wedding.....said no couple ever!

nevitably, there will be something that doesn't go your way. The level of disruption can vary. Examples of a crisis can be vendors pulling out last minute, a loved one not able to attend, running out of money or a global pandemic. Either way here is my mantra;

'There is nothing we can't fix or adapt'.

I have never come across a wedding dilemma that couldn't be sorted or that a plan B can't compensate for. When you plan your wedding with care and follow the steps in previous chapters, the likelihood of you ending up in a dilemma is greatly reduced.

4 C's to adopt in a crisis

Calm

When disaster strikes, keep calm and power through. Sometimes removing yourself from the crisis can do you the world of good. Be purposeful in your quest to seek calm. Take time out and calm the mind.

Consider:

When you are in a calm mindset, you can now start to consider the situation rationally. You may have tasked your bridal party or wedding coordinator with finding a work around. Gather all of the options and review with a clear mindset.

Tip

Allow others to help and you will find that you can approach a crisis with much more power.

Calculate

It is important to understand if there is a financial impact. Is it like Covid 19 where you have to downsize or have to pay for something on the double. Money can be a very powerful stress provoker, getting to grips early means that you can be more objective in solving the problem or getting the assistance you need.

Control

I heard a saying recently….. Control the controllable. Remember this! A crisis tends to be out of your control. Accepting things can go wrong is half the battle. Holding on to that control won't fix the problem. In the words of Elsa from Frozen "Let it Go'.

Chapter Nineteen

Postponing or Downsizing

Changing the format of a wedding can be done with ease most of the time. In 2020, the world was greeted by one of our generations biggest pandemics. The Corona Virus spread throughout the world and in order to protect ourselves, we entered various lockdowns and restrictions. Weddings were impacted greatly and there were many restrictions which resulted in so many being forced to postpone or downsize.

Whatever your circumstances, you've got this and don't panic. I've got some tips to help keep you calm and in order.

Postponement Checklist

The Venue:

- ✓ Contact your venue to see if you can postpone.

- ✓ If you can, gather a selection of dates as more than likely when you go to align all of your key suppliers, one exact date may not suit everyone.

- ✓ You will need to understand all cost implications of changing the date of your wedding. Many venues increase their prices year on year.

- ✓ If you cannot postpone and choose to move to another venue, you may not be entitled to your deposit back. It is important to read the terms of your contract and discuss with the wedding coordinator to ensure that you are crystal clear on yours and the venues contractual obligations.

- ✓ In some cases, the parameters of your contract may change as you could be moving from a non-prime season date to a prime season date or vice versa. In this case price plays a big role. In addition, a venue may have different requirements on minimum numbers and inclusions in packages.

Suppliers & Ceremony:

- ✓ When you have a selection of dates from your venue, the first port of call is to ensure that your priest/registrar or officiant can accommodate your change of date.

- ✓ You will need to update the state of your change. Normally, if your change is within the three to six month time frame, they simply amend the date but should your extension go above six months you will need to notify the state three months before your new date.

- ✓ When you have consensus on dates with your venue and ceremony, you will then move to your suppliers and check their availability.

- ✓ The reality is that not all suppliers will be able to accommodate your change of date.

- ✓ You will need to understand if you are entitled to your deposit back or in some cases given your notice period, do you owe money. In most cases, you won't be entitled to a refund if you cancel.

- ✓ If you have wedding insurance, you may need to extend your policy to align with your new date.

Guests:

- ✓ While you are working through dates with your venue and ceremony officiant, you will also need to be checking dates with your key bridal party to ensure that they are available.

- ✓ Once the new date is confirmed, check in with your stationery vendor for capacity to update your invitations or you may want to source 'Change of Date' notifications.

- ✓ If you have a wedding website, update with your new details.

Finally...Breathe a BIG sigh of relief!

Switching Things Down

Whether it's a change in personal circumstances, a change of heart or an external factor that commands numbers to reduce, you may take to the road of downsizing or eloping.

Should you decide to do either, you need to restructure your day and understand what the new version of events will be. When you initially booked your wedding, you signed many contracts agreeing to host your wedding on a certain day under certain circumstances. If the parameters of this agreement have changed, your first port of call will be to establish the financial or contractual impact. Some venues may not accommodate smaller weddings and may insist that you still pay for the numbers you are contracted for. It is important that you have that first conversation with your venue. In some cases, you may feel so passionately about having a smaller wedding that you are happy to forfeit the deposit and move your wedding to a more intimate setting. Always ask if the venue or supplier can re-sell the date, can you get a percentage of the deposit back. It's a good compromise and many will agree if asked.

Once you have worked on the contractual piece and know exactly where you stand, the next stage is to plan your re-imagined wedding.

Downsizing to a 'Micro-Wedding':

This is exactly what it sounds like, it is reducing the number of your wedding significantly so that it takes a new form.

A micro-wedding is a small intimate affair and can be an absolutely beautiful option. You can retain all of the elements including band, cake, photographer and much more. Couples shouldn't feel that they have to deprive themselves of the key items that make a wedding. The main difference is that you are keeping your guest numbers below fifty people. Most micro-weddings I have seen are roughly 30 people or less. What a micro-wedding allows you to do is deliver on the detail. By detail I refer to signature gourmet menus, ornate floral centrepieces and basically all of the things that are difficult to operationally provide at scale or affordability. Couples can still wear their finery and in some cases, couples may decide to be less formal in their attire. Micro-weddings are a very personal event as it really is your nearest and dearest in attendance.

Typically in Ireland, most wedding venues are built to cater for one hundred or more guests but as we have witnessed during the pandemic, both venues and restaurants adapted well to provide beautiful alternatives for couples wishing to embrace the micro-wedding.

Eloping:

When we hear of eloping, we tend to think of couples running away to Las Vegas to be married by Elvis in the Little White Chapel. An elopement is so much more than that. In fact, on the international arena, Ireland and in particular the West of Ireland, is considered one of the top destinations to elope to. We welcome many international couples every year to our fair isle as they say 'I do' on the Cliffs of Moher.

Eloping tends to be where a couple secretly runaway and get married. Overtime this has evolved and couples let their closest know that they will be eloping.

Couples can opt to elope within their own country and Ireland has some amazing destinations to visit. My personal favourites are the Wild Atlantic Way, Donegal and some of our national parks and forests. There are dedicated companies and officiants in Ireland that specialise in the elopement process. A simple Google search will show options. Should a couple wish to go abroad and elope, again, there are planners on the ground in that country that will coordinate the process and legalities for you.

Chapter Twenty

Stress

As the book draws to an end, I feel that it is so important
to talk about the big S!

S tress is the killer of all excitement in the lead up to a wedding, particularly where there might be drama within the bridal party, fundamental upheaval to the wedding day or you have been let down in some form.

Managing yourself and your own stress levels is a priority as if either of the couple gets overwhelmed, it can lead to getting ill, low energy and in some cases feelings of great anxiety. All of this can cast a shadow over the joy of getting married. So many couples expressed feelings of being burnt out as they approached the big day and paid for it on honeymoon.

Whilst I appreciate it is easier said than done, there are ways to avoid and reduce the feelings and impact of stress.

Sleep

I can't express the importance on getting enough sleep. The experts say a minimum of seven hours is required to function effectively and I know that when I get less than seven hours sleep, I am less productive and have a shorter fuse. Wedding planning and particularly the lead up the a wedding requires a lot of energy so therefore it is so important to recharge the batteries where you can.

Eat

I recall forgetting to eat in those few days before the wedding and at a time when you need all of the good stuff, this is not the time to forget to eat. I was also tired so grabbing quick sugar hits gave me that temporary boost only to feel exhausted later. If I was to do it all again, I would plan my meals and prepare healthy quick pick snacks that I can grab on the go. Eating well will keep you motoring well and the breakouts at bay. I did Weight Watchers for my own bridal prep and by no means am I suggesting that anyone takes this on but what it did give me was the discipline to eat well which carried through…until honeymoon and then the wheels came right off! On the day, you will be busy getting photos and mingling with guests, ask the wedding team at your venue or caterer to set aside a plate of quick snacks for you so that you can take time out, even for five minutes, and refuel. Don't underestimate how much refuelling you will need.

✳ Water

This was my biggest down fall! We should aim to drink two litres of water a day. I know that when I do this, my skin is great and I feel I have more energy. I remember the day before the wedding I just couldn't muster the energy to keep at the pace I was going the previous day. My good friend is a doctor and she looked at my eyes and whatever voodoo power she has by looking at my eyes, she could see that I was dehydrated and sent me off to get that H20 in. It took a few hours for me to feel refreshed so just make a conscious effort to take a few sips every little while. To make it fun, grab yourself a novelty bride or personalised bottle, add limes and lemons to give is a fun taste. A trick I heard is that if you put a straw in your glass of water, you are more likely to keep sipping. Who knows! Just find what works for you and keep that water flowing. A good tip is to ask your wedding coordinator to ensure that a fresh mini bottle of water is dropped to you every few hours. This way, you don't have to worry about remembering, let someone else take that on!

✳ Exercise

Whatever exercise is for you, embrace it. Some of you could be marathon runners and some great walkers. Find something that you can do daily for thirty minutes. I like to go for a brisk walk every day for thirty minutes. I also loved doing couch to 10k when I was in bridal prep mode. You don't have to kill yourself here, just get moving. When we move and increase our heart rate, we also release the good hormones that improve our mood, coping skills and give us more energy.

Visualisation

Sometimes when we get stressed it's because we are pre-empting something bad that might never happen. You may also be experiencing nerves thinking about walking up the aisle, having to do a speech or even having the spotlight on you for the day. Whatever the trigger is for your stress, I find visualising a positive end result the best. I was very nervous and emotional about walking up the aisle. I have no idea why but every time I thought about it I got butterflies in my tummy. I found that thinking positively about the process really helped me talk myself out of the anxiety. Reshape your thinking to tell your brain that those butterflies are excitement and a sign that you can't wait to do the aisle walk or speech. I used to put the song we chose for the aisle on as I went for a walk or jog. Overtime I had visualised a positive outcome so much that it completely reduced my worry about not being able to stop crying in the church. This can work across any area you are worrying about. If you are worried about making the speech, think about the feeling of relief and pride when it is done. If it is an overall sense of worry about everything going well on the day, picture it going well!

Connection

Sometimes I find couples internalise all of the stress of their wedding. It is really important to be able to share the problems or just talk out ideas with those who are involved in your wedding. Keep talking and sharing the problems and you will find that as a team, you can problem solve more effectively.

Delegation

One of the hardest things couples find is understanding all of the tasks that need to be completed and also not being able to let go of the jobs. I recommend delegating early. Look at your wider to-do list and if there are specific tasks that you know will be required closer to and on the day of the wedding, delegate. So many would love to have a role for your wedding day so don't be afraid to delegate to those whom you can trust. If you feel the entire process is very overwhelming, it's never too late to bring in a wedding planner. They can help get you over the final hurdle and coordinate all of the moving parts on the day of the wedding.

☀ Switching off

When I refer to switching off, I mean both digitally and physically. With so much information on social media, it can be information overload and we saw this at its worst during the pandemic. When you feel anxiety building, put the phone away and do something that brings you joy. Make time to turn down the noise in your mind. Whether that's getting out for a walk with friends with no wedding talk or being pampered at a spa, do what you need to just settle your mind. You will feel so much more revived, rational and relaxed when you do this. Treat your mind to a little break.

Tip

The key takeaway here is to mind yourself as you want to be able to enjoy the moment and honeymoon and not feel floored. **Your body and mind is a temple afterall!**

Parting advice

I hope you have found this guide helpful. This is such a special time for you both and it is so important to enjoy it. There will be stressful times but this is just preparation for your healthy married life.

Try to not lose sight of the purpose of your special day and make sure to make time for each other.

Your

Wedding

Checklist

12 months

- Before jumping in to planning, take some time to enjoy the moment
- Discuss what you would both like your wedding day to look like
- Consider funding
- Jot down names of guests to invite to gain an understanding of size of wedding
- Reconsider if this number fits budget and wedding day style (try not to have a tiff at this point!)
- Choose bridal party
- Have an engagement gathering

Book your date sensitive items:

- Book church / registrar or humanist (you will need to balance dates between ceremony and venue)
- Research, visit & book wedding venue
- If planning an abroad wedding, liaise with destination planner and book
- Book photographer
- Book band and DJ
- Book videographer
- Book music for ceremony

9-12 months

- ✳ Choose your wedding dress
- ✳ Order bridesmaids' dresses
- ✳ Book cars / transport
- ✳ Book honeymoon (check and order passports if required)
- ✳ Book florist
- ✳ Discuss with bridal parties what you may like for hen/stag
- ✳ Start hair and facial treatments
- ✳ Buy wedding insurance if you opt for this

6-9 months

- 🌟 Book or buy groom / groomsmen's suits
- 🌟 Book make-up artist (make sure to do a trial!)
- 🌟 Book hairdresser (make sure to do a trial!)
- 🌟 Order invitations and stationery
- 🌟 Order wedding cake
- 🌟 Book pre-marriage course if getting married in a church
- 🌟 Buy wedding rings
- 🌟 Book extras such as candycart, favours, lighting, photobooth etc..

3 - 6
months

* Notify the state of intention to marry and coordinate all paper work
* Confirm church/ceremony booklet content – music, prayers, readings, readers and reflections
* Confirm booklet details with stationery supplier

2-3 months

* Wedding dress should arrive as well as bridesmaids dresses
* Coordinate alterations
* Send invitations
* Select gifts for bridal party
* Confirm flower arrangements with florist

1-2 months

* Contact reception venue with final menu details, approximate numbers
* Contact suppliers to check final arrangements
* Buy accessories

2-4
weeks

* Chase any unanswered RSVPs
* Finalise guest numbers and confirm with
  wedding venue
* Complete table plan
* Prepare honeymoon bag
* Pay final bills to suppliers and confirm arrival times
* Prepare foreign exchange and notify bank of travel
* If getting a loan for your wedding, drawdown funds

1

week

* Collect dresses
* Collect suits
* Prepare bag for wedding night
* Organise to have breakfast delivered to the brides preparation venue (you don't want the smell of a cooked breakfast on your dress!)

24-48 hours

* Go to beauticians for nails, tan, waxing treatments.
  No harm to get a relaxation treatment too!
* Grooms enjoy a shave and barber treatment
* Attend rehearsal for ceremony and rehearsal dinner
* Give rings to the best man (or if nervous, can wait
  until the ceremony!)
* Delegate jobs of returning suits, collecting left over
  cake, bringing flowers from church to venue to
  other bridal party members

Your Wedding Day

- ☀ Following a good nights sleep, wake up excited and refreshed!
- ☀ Have a good breakfast
- ☀ Enjoy getting ready
- ☀ Ensure that someone has water and tissues ready as it is an emotional day
- ☀ Groom to take ceremony booklets to ceremony and give to ushers to hand out
- ☀ Take some time out between photos and reception to have a drink together to enjoy the moment
- ☀ Enjoy the day!

Notes

About
the author

Sara Kennedy is one of Ireland & Northern Ireland's leading and award winning wedding experts and founder of IrishWeddingBlog.ie. Sara is a sought-after event host & contributor, appearing at specialist wedding venues and events throughout the country to share her expertise, honed from her 20 years-experience in the industry.

A regular media contributor across print, digital and broadcast channels, Sara also hosted a regular wedding feature on Virgin Media's Xpose, Ireland Am and RTE Today shows. Sara is author of 'The Ultimate Wedding Planning Guide', which has become essential reading for brides and grooms-to-be in Ireland. More recently, Sara has launched a much loved wedding podcast ' Real Weddings with Sara'

IrishWeddingBlog.ie attracts thousands of visitors every month, as well as its thriving social media following, who are drawn to Sara's no-nonsense approach to wedding planning with particular expertise on DIY wedding design and emphasis on learnings from real weddings.

Acknowledgements

I would like to extend my thanks to so many people who have helped me on this journey.

Firstly, my poor husband who has had endless hours of proof reading so that I could get this over the line. Eoin, I love you so much and thank you for your support. Thank you to James and Adam, you have brought so much happiness to our lives.

Thank you to my parents for the endless support and encouragement. Mam, thank you for your contributions and Dad, I'm sure some day you'll know what a wedding blog is!

The Kennedy gang, thank you for allowing me to unleash my wedding planning obsession, your willingness to always help is a blessing.

My dearest friends and mentors, you all know who you are. Thank you for traipsing around endless wedding fairs.

Sean Egan.....you have the patience of a saint. Your creativity and help has been truly appreciated.

Huge thanks to all of the photographers that supplied images including;

Elaine Barker Photography

Ali and Laura Photography

Roslyn from Couple.ie

Emma Russell

Dasha Caffrey

Magda Lukas

C2 Photo

Jasna Pasalic

Mark Donovan

Pawel Bebenca

Joe Conroy

Peter Rowan

Thank you to the couples that allowed their photographers to share their weddings.

Finally, I could not sign off without thanking the supporters of Irish Wedding Blog, you are all amazing!

Best Wishes,

Sara xx